LEONARD J. ARRINGTON
MORMON HISTORY LECTURE SERIES
NO. 26

T0168118

"A MARVELOUS WORK"

READING MORMONISM
IN WEST AFRICA

by Laurie F. Maffly-Kipp

Sponsored by
Special Collections & Archives
Merrill-Cazier Library
Utah State University
LOGAN

Copyright
All rights reserved.
ISBN 978-1-64642-347-7 (paperback)
ISBN 978-1-64642-348-4 (ebook)
https://doi.org/10.5876/9781646423484

Published by Merrill-Cazier Library
Distributed by Utah State University Press
Logan, UT 84322

FOREWORD

The establishment of a lecture series honoring a library's special collections and a donor to that collection is unique. Utah State University's Merrill-Cazier Library houses the personal and historical collection of Leonard J. Arrington, a renowned scholar of the American West. As part of Arrington's gift to the university, he requested that the university's historical collection become the focus for an annual lecture on an aspect of Mormon history. Utah State University agreed to the request and in 1995 inaugurated the annual Leonard J. Arrington Mormon History Lecture.

Utah State University's Special Collections and Archives is ideally suited as the host for the lecture series. The state's land grant university began collecting records very early and in the 1960s became a major depository for Utah and Mormon records. Leonard and his wife, Grace, joined the Utah State University (USU) faculty and family in 1946, and the Arringtons and their colleagues worked to collect original diaries, journals, letters, and photographs.

Although trained as an economist at the University of North Carolina, Arrington became a Mormon historian of international repute. Working with numerous colleagues, the Twin Falls, Idaho, native produced the classic *Great Basin Kingdom: An Economic History of the Latter-day Saints* in 1958. Utilizing available collections at USU, Arrington embarked on a prolific publishing and editing career. He and his close ally, Dr. S. George Ellsworth, helped organize the Western History Association (WHA), and they created the *Western Historical Quarterly* as the scholarly voice of the WHA. While serving with Ellsworth as editor of the new journal, Arrington also helped establish both the Mormon History Association and the independent journal *Dialogue*.

One of Arrington's great talents was to encourage and inspire other scholars or writers. While he worked on biographies or institutional histories, he employed many young scholars as researchers. He fostered many careers as well as arranged for the publication of numerous books and articles.

In 1972, Arrington accepted appointments as the official historian of the Church of Jesus Christ of Latter-day Saints and the Lemuel Redd Chair of Western History at Brigham Young University (BYU). More and more, Arrington focused on Mormon, rather than economic, historical topics. His own career flourished with the publication of *The Mormon Experience*, coauthored with Davis Bitton, and *American Moses: A Biography of Brigham Young*. He and his staff produced many research papers and position papers for the Church of Jesus Christ of Latter-day Saints as well. Nevertheless, tension developed over the historical process, and Arrington chose to move full time to BYU with his entire staff. The Joseph Fielding Smith Institute of History was established, and Arrington continued to mentor new scholars as well as publish biographies. He also produced a very significant two-volume study, *The History of Idaho*.

After Grace Arrington passed away, Leonard married Harriet Horne of Salt Lake City. They made the decision to deposit the vast Arrington collection of research documents, letters, files, books, and journals at Utah State University. The Leonard J. Arrington Historical Archives is part of the university's Special Collections. The Arrington Lecture Committee works with Special Collections to sponsor the annual lecture.

"A MARVELOUS WORK"

Reading Mormonism in West Africa

In the summer of 1960, Glen T. Fisher, the outgoing mission president of the Church of Jesus Christ of Latter-day Saints (LDS) in South Africa, began the long journey home from the field. Because of the church's long-standing ban on temple work among members of (Black) African descent (often referred to as the "priesthood ban," though it affected both males and females), the South African mission was at that point the only outpost of LDS Church activity on the continent. Established in the 1850s as an outreach to those of European descent, the African mission had kept the evangelization of Black Africans at a cautious arm's length. But beginning in the years after World War II, word filtered back that Christians in Nigeria and Ghana were requesting literature and guidance from church leadership about how to establish Mormon churches in their regions. Reports were sketchy, but some estimates from their correspondents in the West African region placed the numbers of congregants in these unofficial Mormon churches in the thousands. At a loss to know what to do, given the priesthood ban, President David O. McKay commissioned Fisher to stop through on a brief trip and pursue the matter. "Were these potential church members sincere?" he wondered.

Years later, Fisher reminisced about his visit to West Africa, recalling his impressions of the churches in Nigeria that had aligned themselves with the Mormon faith. The communities are very poor, he noted, and the churches had neither seats, musical instruments, nor even a pulpit. "The leader of the group carried his supplies in a wooden box which he used as a pulpit. Supplies consisted of a few Bibles, some missionary pamphlets, the *Articles of Faith* by James E. Talmage, and *A Marvelous Work and a Wonder* by LeGrand Richards." On further inspection, he found the same pattern and the same reading material in other churches. In only one did he spy a copy of the Book of Mormon. "From this literature a church organization had been effected, patterned after the Mormon church."[1]

The same sorts of events were taking place in neighboring Ghana. Joseph Kawme Dadzie, one of the first self-styled Mormons there, wrote to Lamar Williams in the Missionary Department in Salt Lake City in the early 1960s requesting more information about the church. Williams responded and shipped him copies of A *Marvelous Work and a Wonder, Gospel Principles,* and several other books. Around the same time, Raphael A. F. Mensah, a Ghanaian visiting the United Kingdom, received some church pamphlets from Lilian Clark, a woman he had met there. She herself was not a church member, but she gladly shared the literature with him. Mensah, armed with his pamphlets and additional books provided by the missionary department, began preaching about the Mormon faith to his friends and neighbors, eventually forming several congregations of yet-unofficial Mormon churches. In 1964 Mensah was joined by W. J. B. (Billy) Johnson, who teamed up with Mensah in preaching and conducting meetings. Together they founded religious gatherings "of nearly 1,000 members."[2]

What was going on here? And, even more urgently, what could the Church of Jesus Christ of Latter-day Saints, the one in Utah, do to protect its name and guard the boundaries of its beliefs? Christianity, in one sense, has from its beginnings witnessed struggles over who can claim its mantle as the true form of belief. And the Salt Lake–based church in 1960, having worked for decades to assure its status as a legitimate American religious tradition, and focusing its international efforts on standardization of doctrines and practices, did not want to see its hard efforts threatened by "renegade" believers assuming its name.

Even more concerning to the church leaders was that word had spread beyond Salt Lake City about the West African self-styled Mormons. In June 1965 *Time* magazine published a brief article about the phenomenon. Its author recounted that from the early 1950s, circulating books and tracts had been sent from church headquarters to Nigerian seekers. By latest count, these Mormon churches had seventy-five elders and branches in six cities. Estimates at that time put their numbers at approximately 10,000 baptized adults and 6,000 children. All this phenomenal growth had occurred without benefit of US-based LDS missionaries, since the

Nigerian government would not grant them resident visas. As the widely circulated magazine pointed out, in the absence of US oversight, the Nigerian Mormons had established their own "black hierarchy, priests and all." Anie Dick Obot, the bishop presiding over the Nigerian elders, responded to questions about the legitimacy of this church structure by asserting that he did not "have to wait for revelation to know that I am the natural head in Nigeria . . . Nigerian priests will run their own branch. This is their creation, and they are in their own country."[3]

All these events are interesting in and of themselves, and historians such as James B. Allen, Russell Stevenson, Greg Prince, and Dmitri Hurlbut have provided rich detail about the anxieties expressed by President McKay, Glen Fisher, Lamar Williams, and other LDS Church leaders in this era. They have analyzed why West Africans might have found their church a desirable home and how transatlantic negotiations were shaped by the politics of race within the US domestic context. My concern here relates to these developments, but it also attempts to shift our focus onto the self-styled Mormons themselves. I hope this will allow us to better understand not the *why* of conversion, but the *how*. How did West Africans in this era fashion collective religious systems out of textual fragments and personal testimony? Thus, this is less an institutional story—though it is related to institutions—and more an exploration of the lived faith as experienced by those "on the ground." What did this self-styled Mormonism look like, and how did believers craft churches out of the bare materials of tracts and inspirational volumes? This talk explores the circulation and interpretation of this homegrown Mormon faith in the 1960s and 1970s and concludes with the dilemmas raised by this religious self-fashioning for LDS Church establishment after 1978. In other words, what does it mean to "read" Mormonism in West Africa?

But it is also a story about "reading" in another sense. Utah church leaders were also trying to decipher first the intentions, and later the religious practices, of West African Mormons. In this regard, they were shaped as much by their own domestic context as were their transatlantic counterparts. They understood their exchanges with Nigerians and Ghanaians through the lenses of racial politics in the United States, as well as through their own aspirations for acceptance on the American religious scene.

One more word by way of clarification and introduction. Throughout my remarks I use the terms "Mormon" and "Mormonism," and I do so for at least two reasons. First, this is a historical exploration, and these were the terms used at the time. The two most well-known circulating texts sent to West Africa that I mentioned a bit earlier were James E. Talmage, *Articles of Faith*, and LeGrand Richards's *A Marvelous Work and a Wonder*. Both authors consistently use these terms to describe their faith and enjoin others to embrace the description. Talmage, one of the most prolific LDS writers of the twentieth century, published multiple volumes with the term "Mormonism" in the title, referring to the faith that he sought to explain and defend. LeGrand Richards's work, in turn, was originally published in the 1930s as a series of lessons for missionaries entitled "The Message of Mormonism." In turn, these are the terms that came to West Africa in those original shipments of pamphlets and books, and they most accurately capture the identities embraced by believers there. Second, I also use these terms because we are describing here multiple traditions under a "Mormon" tent. Obviously, there has been and continues to be contestation over which traditions are legitimate, authorized, or correct. It is precisely this contestation that is part of our story.

Understanding self-styled Mormonism in this era requires that we begin with the stories of believers. Anthony Uzodimma Obinna described his journey to Mormon faith in his own words. Born in 1928 in southeastern Nigeria, Obinna was an ethnic Igbo whose family observed traditional Igbo customs, including the practice of polygamy. In his recollections, Obinna explains that his people "detested Western education and hated anyone who talked to them about sending their children to school or taking them to church." Nonetheless, as the fifth of twenty-four children, he was sent to school to learn English, after which he became a teacher. His studies continued with correspondence courses from Oxford, England in English, geography, economics, and history.[4]

Beginning in the mid-1960s, Obinna explains that he had a series of dreams. In the first one, he encountered a tall man in white shorts who asked him whether he knew about Christianity, and specifically about Christian and Christiana in John Bunyan's *The Pilgrim's Progress*. He replied that he had read it but had forgotten it, so the man told him to reread it. Several months later, in another dream, the "personage" took him to a "most beautiful building" and showed him "everything in it." The man appeared to him three times in all. Several years later, Obinna continues, placing his account during the Nigerian Civil War of the late 1960s, he picked up an old copy of the *Reader's Digest* for September 1958, and opened it to find a picture of the building from his dream that accompanied an article, "The March of the Mormons."[5]

"From the time I finished reading the story," he recalled, "I had no rest of mind any longer. My whole attention was focused on my new discovery. I rushed out immediately to tell my brothers, who were all amazed and astonished to hear the story." Compelled by his dreams and the remarkable coincidence of this image, Obinna also wrote to LDS Church headquarters, requesting instructions and more literature. And here began his journey in the Mormon faith, which would culminate after 1978 into his baptism into the Church of Jesus Christ of Latter-day Saints.[6]

Obinna's story is perhaps the best-known account from this era, but it is far from the only one. Lamar Williams, who worked in the Church Missionary Department in the early 1960s, recalled receiving over 1,000 letters from West Africans requesting literature during this period. Along with Glen Fisher's brief visit, Williams also visited West Africa several times in the first years of the decade, but brief, sporadic site visits from Utah could not provide the sustained attention needed to re-create an official version of church practice on African soil. By default, the readiest conduit for information about Mormon teachings was through pamphlets and popularized interpretations of the faith.

But the combination of distance and inability to embark on sustained missionary activity was not the only reason for disconnection. Language, education, and lack of resources also played important roles. Although English was the official language of both Nigeria and Ghana by virtue of their history as colonial possessions of Great Britain, it was typically not the first language of Indigenous peoples. Instead, they tended to learn some rudimentary English in school, but their primary languages were determined by localized tribal groups—Twi, Ga, Ewe, Ibibo, or one of many other regional groupings.

This basic fissure of language capabilities had multiple implications for self-styled Mormons who picked up books to learn about the faith. Most fundamentally, it meant that Mormonism was a religion initially passed along by people, such as Anthony Obinna, who exercised a high degree of English literacy. In the years following Ghanaian independence in 1957, the state established a program of universal education, much of which was provided through religious organizations such as Methodist or Catholic schools. Ebow Ghartney, another early self-styled Mormon, observed that these schools were still steeped in the educational systems of British colonialism, and thus they placed great emphasis on the humanities and traditions of British literature. Many of the first local Mormon leaders were trained in these settings and thereby were provided with comprehensive education in English texts. They were encouraged to continue their education in Europe or the United States, thereby solidifying their skills in both the English language and the values of western societies. It is no wonder, then, that Obinna's revelation, and the message from his spiritual visitor to reread John Bunyan's classic Puritan text, *The Pilgrim's Progress*, resonated so deeply and propelled him toward the church. It linked his previous immersion in texts with revelations of a Mormon future.[7]

The experiences of Ebenezer Owusu-Ansah emphasize just how deeply the love of reading as a form of religious enthusiasm motivated the early self-styled Mormons in West Africa. Owusu-Ansah was from Kumasi, in the Ashanti region of Ghana (traditionally a majority Muslim area). He described himself as a voracious reader, who, at the age of sixteen, began reading about all sorts of religious traditions. He was confused about which was the "true church" (note the parallels to accounts of Joseph Smith Jr.'s first vision). Finally, he began reading the Bible, and he read straight through from Genesis through Isaiah. Still, he hadn't found the answer to his question, so he moved on to the New Testament. It was only when he reached the book of Revelation and the prophecies of the Second Coming that his interest was piqued. He claims to have read that book multiple times.[8]

While he did not join a church in this period, he finally met up with some missionaries (he thought "they were twins" because they had suits with name tags). They read aloud to him from the Book of Mormon (Mosiah 3:3–11), and he recalls that he was "touched" by it. "So really I'm a convert of the Book of Mormon. I was converted by what I read in the Book of Mormon." After joining the church, he was determined to read all the institute manuals and as much other church literature as he could get his hands on. After his stint at the Missionary Training Center (MTC) he vowed to read the Book of Mormon twenty-four times during the following two years—he claims that instead he read it twenty-five times. As of 1998, he claimed to have read the book up to forty-three times. "I can't get along without the book."[9]

These experiences also point to a second feature of early West African interest in Mormonism. It was deeply and indelibly shaped by prior familiarity with the Bible. As Ebow Ghartney put it, "Almost all of us were

Christians before. I've known Bible stories all my life, and a lot of people have, so it makes sense in our culture." In reading through the letters of West Africans to Lamar Williams in the Missionary Department, one enters a world that is utterly saturated with biblical phrasing, images, and metaphors. The Reverend Udo-Ete, writing to Lamar Williams in 1960, sprinkled his letters with scriptural verses. He did not so much quote the Bible as he referenced it, citing "Acts 16:9" or "Daniel 2:3," assuming that his reader would readily understand his shorthand. This style indicates just how thoroughly steeped in the world of the Bible many West Africans were and are, to this day. Udo-Ete was himself the founder of a Christian church, the Prayer Church Mission, and his stylistic use of the Bible, along with his frequent interjections in his writings of "Amen" and "praise the Lord," also suggest the charismatic, or spirit-filled, nature of his faith.[10]

The biblical focus of West African cultures also meant that believers measured the worth of the Book of Mormon by how it measured up to their interpretations of the Bible—just as was true among the first Mormon converts in the antebellum United States. Juliana Amoah-Kpentey, when asked what led to her Mormon faith, recalled that initially she "hated this Church *because* of the Book of Mormon. I said, 'I don't like any church that uses two Bibles at the same time,' so I didn't like this Church." It wasn't until she visited, and perhaps more important, when she recognized the similarities of the stories of the Book of Mormon to those in the Bible, that she changed her mind. She described how the missionaries she later met would read alternate passages in the two books, and eventually she realized "they are all the same thing, so I realized it was a good book." However, she also commented that she hadn't really "studied it much." Amoah-Kpentey, like other Bible-believing West Africans, measured the truth of Mormonism by the yardstick of the Bible—but this sometimes served as an initial impediment to accepting it. Mormonism, in other words, had to measure up.[11]

There is, in fact, relatively little mention of the Book of Mormon among early self-styled church members. The reasons for this are relatively straightforward. If language was a barrier for many who lacked facility in English, it is likely that the Book of Mormon, with its language that draws on the King James–style phrasing, proved an even more impenetrable text. Grant Hardy has argued persuasively that the idioms and archaic word forms of the King James Bible are difficult for many native English speakers to grasp, much less people with only a moderate command of the language. While he concedes that the King James Bible is "too deeply rooted" in LDS history and "too connected to latter-day revelations to simply abandon," its exclusive usage can be an impediment to the acceptance of the faith. The West Africans, who at the time were less literate in their own written languages, then, would have had to do a double translation, since the Book of Mormon was not available in their native tongues.[12]

Indeed, the Book of Mormon was barely physically available to them at all in written form, despite the best efforts of Lamar Williams to ship off hundreds of materials to his correspondents. And church members in West Africa were in no financial position to buy and ship their own books. When BYU professor and businessman Lynn Hilton made a visit to Cape Coast, Ghana, in 1969, he met with self-styled Mormon church members who had heard he would be in the country and sought him out. They showed him their modest church building: "It was a mud architecture building, only one story high," Hilton remembered. "And there was a sign over the door that said, 'Church of Jesus Christ of Latter-day Saints, Accra, Ghana Branch.' . . . They took us inside and there were rough lumber benches. A dirt floor as I recall." They also showed Hilton their single, well-used copy of the Book of Mormon. "You could tell that literally thousands of people had gone through that book and licked their fingers," Hilton said. "All the corners were rounded and dark colored and so dog-eared that the pages fanned out . . . The cover of the book was actually standing." His hosts explained to him that each person was allowed just a few minutes with the book, then it was passed on to the next person to read; the book, they said, was being "used and read around the clock and week after week."[13]

Early church members from the 1960s and early 1970s comment more frequently on hearing stories from the Book of Mormon retold by the more educated church leaders, who would make their readings decipherable to those unable to decipher the complex English. Joseph Kawme Dadzie joined another self-styled Mormon church under the direction of Rebecca Mould in the late 1960s in Cape Coast. He recalled that Mould would not read from the Book of Mormon, but she "occasionally talked about" it and described its origins. She would also refer to biblical prophecies that presaged the Book of Mormon, and would read from the Bible, thereby enabling her listeners to bring together biblical teachings with the Mormon testament of Jesus Christ. Kawme Dadzie also noted that "anybody who could read and understand the gospel was given the chance to preach."[14]

The lack of resources, still the case today in many smaller towns and villages in West Africa, dramatically circumscribed how Mormonism was communicated and disseminated. Dadzie's recollections also point to a final reality of the language barrier imposed in the early years of self-styled West African Mormonism. Simply put, for those who wanted to read about the tradition (which most did, since that was one of few conduits to information about the faith), it was much easier to understand what was written about it in *Look Magazine, Reader's Digest*, the *Improvement Era*, or the words of James Talmage or LeGrand Richards, than it was to understand the Book of Mormon or Doctrine and Covenants straight from the English-language versions. Written in simpler language, and often even a folksy manner, these works were geared toward broader audiences.

It should not surprise us to see James Talmage's and LeGrand Richards's works showing up in even the unlikeliest of places; theirs were the top two best-selling books in the history of the Church of Jesus Christ of Latter-day Saints outside of the standard works and were expressly made for missionary activity. Talmage's *Articles of Faith* has gone through over fifty English-language editions alone since 1899. Richards's *A Marvelous Work and a Wonder*, long a staple of the approved missionary library, has sold upwards of 3 million copies and has appeared in several dozen languages. Indeed, some observers have quipped that LeGrand Richards (1886–1983) brought more people to the Mormon faith than any other church member of the twentieth century. He was a missionary at heart, having served in the Netherlands from 1905–8 and returned there as presiding elder during the First World War. After that he rose swiftly through the church system, being tasked by the leadership to serve as the Hollywood stake president (1931–33) and the presiding president over the Southern States Mission (1934–37). It was during his tour in the southern United States that he composed his most notable work, a series of lessons for missionaries that he later revised as *A Marvelous Work and a Wonder* (1950).[15]

More surprising, perhaps, was the popularity of the *Improvement Era* and *Reader's Digest* articles among West Africans. Mentions of the *Reader's Digest* appear to focus on one article in particular, the 1958 piece that Anthony Obinna referred to as the "March of the Mormons" but whose actual title was "The Mormon Church: A Complete Way of Life." You'll recall that Obinna was astonished that the building shown within that article had appeared to him in a dream; it was because of this miraculous coincidence that he knew Mormonism was the correct religion for him. Adewole Ogunmokun, in Port Harcourt, reported a similar response to the same article. After reading it, he recalled, "I became transformed and for a number of days I dreamt dreams of various degrees about the Mormon Church, I have even worshipped in the Great Temple with thousands of other Brethren on more than one occasion, until I became convinced that I was not only dreaming but seen visions of new hope coming to my nation and Africa as a whole through the Mormon church."[16]

The author of that article, Hartzell Spence, was an experienced journalist and author of books that brought romantic historical narratives, pride in American military and corporate success, and models of upstanding religious communities to broader reading audiences. One reviewer characterized his work on the discovery of the Amazon as an "idealistic, adventurous thrilling tale." The son of a Methodist preacher from Iowa, Spence promoted all the values of patriotism, democracy, and free enterprise that infused 1950s American life, and he approached the successes of the Mormons with the same wonder and admiration. Similarly, the *Improvement Era* of the late 1950s and early 1960s reflected a nearly exclusive focus on national, regional, and local success. Its pages also promoted church teachings, yes. But it is the unstated elements of its pages that are most intriguing for our purposes. In images of blonde, blue-eyed families, in subject matter regarding American domestic patterns and consumption, and in the advertising localized to the Mormon culture region, these journals give little indication of how Mormonism might be lived out in urban settings, much less in developing nations.[17]

Now, I admit that it would be easy to view some of these issues as outdated, looking back from the vantage of more than a half century. As we regard them from our post–Vietnam War, vantage, in which we are more complexly questioning institutional and individual racism, these images look intensely parochial, unvaryingly white, and entirely uncritical about the complexities of American exceptionalism. Yet the fact remains that when Lamar Williams showed up in West Africa in 1961, having toted his flannel board for teaching purposes across the Atlantic Ocean, he finally met with one of his correspondents, Honesty John Ekong. Ekong, he described, lived in a mud hut, and his walls were decorated with clippings from the *Improvement Era* and pictures of the General Authorities.[18]

This brings us again to the question: What did these people "read" in Mormonism? What did it offer to them? What was its promise? And how did they find its meaning within the pages of periodical literature, missionary texts and sometimes secondhand interpretations of difficult texts written in languages they barely knew?

I think the answer to these questions is complex, and it cannot be entirely explained without understanding not just the Mormonism they were receiving in books and pamphlets, but the religious and political context in which they lived. Remember that church leaders back in Utah were also trying to "read" this new Mormonism, through the few signs they had available to them in the mail requests arriving wanted to know whether the West Africans who were writing to them were "sincere." They worried that perhaps they were only looking for financial support, or some other sort of handout, rather than authentic faith. Church leaders were skeptical, worried because, as Marvin Jones said, "It is so hard to tell what their underlying motives are. Sincerity or the want of finance."[19]

But West Africans lived in an environment in which "authentic faith" was deeply embedded in gestures of material reciprocity and visions of worldly success. The Bible spoke to Christians in this region as a book that promised abundance and victory. Paul Gifford, one of the foremost scholars of Christianity in Ghana, reminds us that Ghana was the first independent nation in sub-Saharan Africa. Although the country was already very Christianized (some 60% of the population claims to be Christian) with sizable numbers of Roman Catholics, mainline Protestants, Pentecostals, and African Independent Churches—the face of Christianity changed rapidly in the years after independence and underwent a "radical modernization" centered on prayer, faith healing, and prosperity. This new charismatic faith was multinational and drew for support from young leaders trained in theology, and supported by organizations in the United States. That material ballast has been crucial in the face of extreme poverty. "This Christianity is about success," Gifford explains, especially in finance and material achievement. It is led by charismatic leaders, self-styled "prophets" who are specially anointed; they rely on their followers for money and in turn help their congregants in times of need.[20]

We see an example of this in the life and work of one of the most successful charismatic Christian preachers of the last few decades, Benson Andrew Idahosa (1938–1998), also known as the "Father of Pentecostalism in Nigeria." Idahosa founded the Church of God Mission International in 1968, and immediately the movement began spreading through affiliation with church bodies in surrounding countries. Thirty years later, the Church of God Mission was reported to be one of the six largest churches in the world with approximately 7 million members. Idahosa also benefited greatly from affiliation with US churches. He briefly attended the Christ for the Nations

Institute in 1971, an independent Pentecostal college in Dallas, Texas, and later received generous financial support from well-known independent Pentecostal preachers in the United States, including his mentors Gordon and Freda Lindsay, healing evangelist T. L. Osborne, and televangelist Jim Bakker. The church also operates the All Nations for Christ Bible Institute, probably the most popular and influential Bible school in West Africa, one that sends out preachers to plant new independent Pentecostal churches throughout West Africa.[21]

At the same time, West Africans, newly independent from a British colonial past, were also forging new political futures for themselves, in a world in which superpowers, and alliances, held the key to continued success. Dmitri Hurlbut has pointed out that new African nations needed allies with whom to affiliate, and seeking affiliation and support was a common social tool in postindependence West Africa.[22]

All these features, then, may help us to look at the letters written to Lamar Williams and others in a different light. Many West African writers, indeed, use the words "affiliation" and "material support" to describe their goal. Udo-Ete put it this way: "In fact, that was what we want. That is, to affiliating our Church Group with a Truthful mission's board whose entire seeking it to do the full will of God." Honesty John Ekong even stressed that if the Utah church could not help them, perhaps they could refer them to someone else: "Please dear brother in Christ. Kindly refer us to some other missionary bodies over there for affiliation." This is not to say that West Africans were not earnestly looking for a true set of doctrines or a correct church in terms of their beliefs. But it does imply that they did not separate material abundance and authentic faith in quite the way that Utah church leaders understood or could respond to. And it suggests, moreover, that the letters reaching out to the LDS Church may not have been the only letters sent from West African church leaders, who sought partnerships for both their growing church bodies as well as their new national project. During an inrush of US missionary groups in the postcolonial era, Africans saw these groups as potential allies in the many material, political, and religious struggles that they faced.[23]

Another important consideration in understanding these letters is the recognition that West Africans did not necessarily hold the same views about church exclusivity that LDS church members did. West African Christians tended to move freely among Christian churches, seeing their affiliation as a way to align with communities that offered the most promising collaborations. They needed schools, buildings, and books. And ministers needed a living, which they hoped such partnerships might provide. Yet tribal and familial connections were so closely tied to religious identities that conversion to a new church did not necessarily mean renunciation of what had come before; one could ill afford to give up any friends during a storm. R.A.F. Mensah, one of the first converts in Ghana, was raised in a household surrounded by both Christian and Ahmadiyya relations. (Ahmadiyya is a form of Islam that begin in late nineteenth-century India; it tends to be spirit-filled and features a strong belief in angels and revelations, much like the charismatic Christian churches in West Africa at the time.) Mensah eventually converted to Methodism, then joined the Seventh-day Adventists. According to Russell Stevenson, Mensah affiliated with many churches but never abandoned any of the churches he associated with. In similar fashion, Juliana Amoah-Kpentey grew up in an Apostolic Pentecostal Church, the Divine Healing Church of Christ, then moved to the Medieval Church Mission. Only after that did she join the Church of Jesus Christ of Latter-day Saints. These patterns of serial affiliation, or multiple affiliation, were extremely common among early West African Mormons.[24]

At the same time, Utah leaders read their interactions with West Africans through the lens of their own domestic concerns. Lamar Williams had planned a return trip to Nigeria in November 1962, but racial politics back home delayed it. George Romney was running a campaign for the governorship of Michigan, and church officials were worried that if Williams embarked on a tour and began baptizing Black African church members, it might be seen as an attempt to help Romney's campaign for governor. Two years later an African newspaper, the *Nigerian Outlook*, published a piece by a Nigerian visiting California. Apparently, he had visited an LDS ward and started to do some research on the temple ban; in response he sent a scathing letter back to Nigeria, excoriating the Mormons for their racism that he likened to South African apartheid. For US church leaders, the issue was domestic and localized, and this press jeopardized their work among African Americans back home. While they had yet to see this as an international, even a pan-African, form of racial protest in which Nigerians were struggling to make their claims in a postcolonial environment, clearly some West Africans framed it this way. As a result, Utah leaders pulled back once again on outreach to Nigeria, and Lamar Williams waited still longer to visit his African correspondents.[25]

These readings and misreading of intent across fragmented lines of communication, in sum, meant that the self-styled Mormon churches that arose in West Africa in the 1960s took on a decidedly localized flavor. They were inflected by the spirit-filled worship of Pentecostal influences, a movement that was becoming increasingly popular in Ghana and Nigeria. They were hopeful for the material and spiritual promises of affiliation with US religion organizations. Those members who joined tended to welcome the potential of American "cultural capital" to help them gain power within their own communities. As for religious practices, they embraced and lived out biblical language but knew only the rudimentary details of the Book of Mormon and rarely quoted it. In the absence of direct guidance from Utah church members to standardize or correlate their teachings, they freely brought in charismatic practices to worship services, including dancing, singing, and extended prayers. Angelina Adjaye recalled her aunt and uncle, who joined a congregation led by Rebecca Mould. She described singing, clapping, and dancing in worship services punctuated by songs about Moroni sung in local languages.[26]

There would be a reckoning in 1978, and a campaign to retranslate the American Mormon tradition in West African settings. The dancing, drumming, and clapping were "regularized." The Utah-based church decided rebaptisms needed to take place under the guidance of American missionaries. Ironically, those adaptations that allowed self-styled Mormonism to endure for nearly twenty years without American oversight were precisely those that needed to be extirpated for global affiliation to take place. West Africans had to choose between fully joining the Utah-based church and giving up local practices or moving to a different religious community. Many chose the latter. Angelina Adjaye's grandmother rejoined the Methodist Church, while her grandfather became a leader in his Ghanaian ward.

Most notably, alongside the cessation of charismatic practices, was the changed role of women leaders. Rebecca Mould had been known by her followers as "Prophetess Rebecca," conforming to traditional patterns of women's authority in southern Ghanaian society. The first constitution of her self-styled Mormon church in 1969 made no mention of gender differences in terms of the priesthood, and women in this church and others like it led prayer groups and performed ritual cleansings and baptisms for both male and female congregants. At times, female authority was questioned: in 1972, male leaders discussed a proposal to bar women from "giving revelations and prophecies." They did not pursue this option but instead instructed those dreams and revelations had to be reported to the pastor. Prophetess Rebecca was elected to a national "high council" of twelve apostles in 1972 with no dissent.[27]

The arrival of LDS missionaries in 1978 required delicate negotiation with this church leader, who also happened to own the building in which the congregation met. Initially, Rebecca welcomed the LDS missionaries and was one of the first baptized into the young Church of Jesus Christ of Latter-day Saints. President Spencer W. Kimball sent along a special commendation to her, and she was set apart as Relief Society president. Her title was changed to "Mother Rebecca," although many followers continued to call her a prophetess and she continued to occupy a prime seat on the dais in the front of the meeting house. Still, efforts to nudge her out of a position of spiritual authority began to chafe, and her leadership became less visible. The missionaries explained to her that the baptisms she had performed were not valid because they had to be conducted by a member of the priesthood. When the missionaries departed in late 1979, arguments broke out in the church as several male members tried to convince her to donate her building to the church. When she refused, she was accused of "abusing" the presidency, and soon thereafter she left the church to reclaim the title of independent church leader.[28]

While her role as Prophetess Rebecca was relatively unusual, the circumstances surrounding her departure suggest that she was far from alone in wanting to retain women's ecclesiastical authority in the church. Her sister, Comfort Mould, had already split away and formed her own charismatic congregation. When Rebecca left the LDS Church, she took a substantial number of her followers with her and continued to use LDS church materials. She continued to consider herself a Mormon. "The Lord knows that I'm a Mormon ... In my heart, I'm a Mormon; I'm a Latter-day Saint."[29]

Notes

1. Alexander B. Morrison, *The Dawning of a Brighter Day: The Church in Black Africa* (Salt Lake City: Deseret Book Company, 1990), 84.
2. Joseph Kawme Dadzie, transcript of oral history, October 15, 1999, Takoradi, Ghana, interviewed by Matthew K. Heiss, Church History Library, OH 2248, 6; Russell Stevenson, "To Recognize One's Face in That of a Foreigner: The Latter-day Saint Experience in West Africa," *The Palgrave Handbook of Global Mormonism*, ed. R. Gordon Shepherd, A. Gary Shepherd, and Ryan T. Cragun (Cham, Switzerland, 2020), 593.
3. "Mormons: The Black Saints of Nigeria," *Time Magazine*, 85, no. 25 (June 18, 1965), http://content.time.com/time/subscriber/article/0,33009,898887,00.html; James B. Allen,

"Would-Be Saints: West Africa before the 1978 Priesthood Revelation," *Journal of Mormon History* 17, no. 1 (1991): 234.

4. Anthony Uzodimma Obinna, "Voice from Nigeria," *Ensign* (December 1980), https://www .churchofjesuschrist.org/study/ensign/1980/12/voice-from-nigeria?lang=eng; David Dmitri Hurlbut, "The 'Conversion' of Anthony Obinna to Mormonism: Elective Affinities, Socio-Economic Factors, and Religious Change in Postcolonial Southeastern Nigeria," *Religions* 11, no. 7 (2020): 358. https://doi.org/10.3390/rel11070358.

5. Obinna, "Voice from Nigeria."

6. Obinna, "Voice from Nigeria."

7. Ebow Ghartney, transcript of oral history, Accra, Ghana, September 13, 1998, interview by Matthew K. Heiss, https://catalog.churchofjesuschrist.org/record/d0d78eae-78d9-4a0c-88ce -7a53a06c49ff/0?view=summary, 9.

8. Ebenezer Owusu-Ansah, transcript of oral history, 3.

9. Ebenezer Owusu-Ansah, transcript of oral history, 4, 12, 24.

10. Ebow Ghartney, transcript of oral history, 13; "Letters from Udo-Ete, Opobo District, Nigeria, 1960 November-1961 March," in LaMar S. Williams Papers, 1959–62, Church History Library, https://catalog.churchofjesuschrist.org/assets/ac5ae736-71e4-4a2c-a1b5 -167f506f3225/0/6.

11. Juliana Amoah-Kpentey transcript of oral history, Accra, Ghana, September 13, 1998, by Matthew K. Heiss, https://catalog.churchofjesuschrist.org/record/79e4ab2d-31be-4dcf-b843 -2e4913c766bc/0?view=summary, 2, 3.

12. Grant Hardy, "The King James Bible and the Future of Missionary Work," *Dialogue: A Journal of Mormon Thought*, 45, no. 2 (Summer 2012): 29.

13. Elizabeth Maki, "A People Prepared: West African Pioneer Preached the Gospel before Missionaries," April 21, 2013, https://history.churchofjesuschrist.org/article/ghana-pioneer-jwb -johnson?lang=eng.

14. Joseph Kawme Dadzie, transcript of oral history, October 15, 1999, Takoradi, Ghana, interviewed by Matthew K. Heiss, Church History Library, OH 2248, 4–5.

15. On Richards's work and influence, see D. Michael Quinn, "They Served: The Richards Legacy in the Church," *Ensign* (January 1980), https://www.churchofjesuschrist.org/study/ensign /1980/01/they-served-the-richards-legacy-in-the-church?lang=eng; Lucile C. Tait, *LeGrand Richards: Beloved Apostle* (Salt Lake City, 1982).

16. Allen, "Would-Be Saints," 214.

17. On Hartzell Spence, see *A Foot in the Door: The Life Appraisal of the Fuller Brush Man* (New York, 1962).

18. Allen, "Would-Be Saints," 218, 225.

19. Marvin R. Jones diary, October 24, 1961, quoted in Stevenson, "To Recognize One's Face in That of a Foreigner," 591.

20. Paul Gifford, "A View of Ghana's New Christianity," in *The Changing Face of Christianity: Africa, the West, and the World*, ed. Lamin Sanneh and Joel A. Carpenter (New York, 2005), 81–94.

21. Usman I. Habib, "A New Paradigm of Leadership Development: Church of God Mission International," PhD diss. (University of Manchester, 2014), chs. 2–3, 6.

22. Hurlbut, "The LDS Church and the Problem of Race: Mormonism in Nigeria, 1946–1978," *International Journal of African Historical Studies*, 51, no. 1 (2018): 6–8.

23. "Letters from Udo-Ete," February 19, 1961; Honesty John Ekong, October 12, 1959, "Reverend Honesty John Ekong Letters from Nigeria, 1959 October–1961 July," Church History Library, MS 2015; Stevenson, "To Recognize One's Face in That of a Foreigner," 596.

24. Russell Stevenson, "Raphael Abraham Frank Mensah (1924–1990s)," (November 2016), BlackPast.org, https://www.blackpast.org/global-african-history/people-global-african -history/mensah-raphael-abraham-frank-1924-1990s/.

25. D. Dmitri Hurlbut, "Nigerian Converts, Mormon Missionaries, and the Priesthood Revelation: Mormonism in Nigeria, 1946–1978," Working Papers in African Studies, Boston University (2015), 8.

26. Angelina M. Adjaye, transcript of oral history, November 7, 2005, Accra, Ghana, interviewed by Clinton D. Christenson, https://catalog.churchofjesuschrist.org/record/2b5a72c3-708b-4fa2-b7b2-e4b676374d62/0?view=browse.

27. For an excellent analysis of Rebecca Mould's congregation, see Russell Stevenson, "'We Have Prophetesses': Mormonism in Ghana, 1964–1979," *Journal of Mormon History* 41, no. 3 (July 2015): 221–57.

28. Stevenson, "We Have Prophetesses," 254–55.

29. J.W.B. Johnson, n.d., interview transcript, Church History Library, OH 4021, 37.